WISEBLOOD ESSAYS IN CONTEMPORARY CULTURE NO. 16

JANE AUSTEN'S DARKNESS

JULIA YOST

WISEBLOOD BOOKS

2024

WISEBLOOD BOOKS
Joshua Hren, Editor-in-Chief
Post Office Box 870
Menomonee Falls, WI 53052
www.wisebloodbooks.com

ISBN: 978-1-963319-84-2

For my father

Jane Austen died in August 1817 at the age of forty-one, four months after laying aside her last manuscript, the first twelve chapters of a satire on healthy people who pretend to be sick. Her recorded symptoms suggest Hodgkin's lymphoma. As early as 1813, she had suffered from back pain, pruritus, neuralgia, night fevers, and anemia causing weakness and discoloration of the face. She endured to compose another masterpiece or three. She was evidently the very opposite of a hypochondriac. "Aunt Jane's health," reports Caroline Austen, "began to fail some time before we knew she was really ill."[1]

"Aunt" is a title that sticks to a spinster. James Edward Austen-Leigh's *A Memoir of Jane Austen* (1869) canonized Aunt Jane as a demure personage who charmed children, though she had none of her own, and whose novels were "the genuine home-made article," intended as family entertainments and only incidentally for publication. Their scope was narrow, their humor genial, and they contained not artistry but "the unadorned reflection of the natural object."[2] Jane, her sister Cassandra, and their widowed mother made up a precarious and dependent household. Jane was the least of these, a spinster like her sister, but rated less highly for her abilities. From this family prejudice it is hard to extricate the somewhat

---

1. Caroline Austen, *My Aunt Jane Austen: A Memoir* (Hampshire: Jane Austen Society, 1991), 13.

2. J. E. Austen-Leigh, *A Memoir of Jane Austen*, 10th ed. (New York: Macmillan, 1906), 108, 144.

condescending "Aunt Jane" persona—which, however, has proved acceptable to many readers for whom her novels are the productions of a gentle observer who aimed to please. Others feel that she aimed to kill. It is possible to view Austen's novels as animated by disgust with the selfish, obtuse, middling, or vicious people who dominate in families and society at the expense of the meritorious, and as haunted by the realities of precarity and poverty, sickness and death, that such people scant or exploit.

In a novel with a marriage plot, we naturally expect to encounter a meritorious heroine whose nuptials will revise her fortunes in accord with our estimation of her. So powerful is our desire for this resolution, we find it even where it is not. In Austen's novels, merit is not, as a rule, rewarded. Romantic love is often costly; nor does it always coincide with the acquisition of self-knowledge or accession to a deserved place in society. Even merit has its dark side, in the temptations of cynicism and misanthropy, which assail the morally intelligent person and turn pride from a virtue to a vice. Marriage is the heroine's only defense against darkness, and with one sparkling exception, it is an uncertain one.

I

Northanger Abbey (1817) ties the beginning of Austen's career to its end. It is an artifact of her juvenilia, which she brushed up in the 1810s but left in the drawer. It appeared posthumously with *Persuasion*, as she appears never to have judged it ready for publication, a judgment comprehensible in view of her standards. It is an unwieldy hybrid, part comedy of manners, part Gothic spoof. Ingenuous Catherine Morland, daughter of a clergyman, meets the nouveau riche Tilney family in Bath and is taken with the good-natured and charming Henry. During a stay with them at their country house, Catherine eagerly constructs the patriarch, General Tilney, as a Gothic villain out of *The Castle of Otranto* and fancies that he murdered his wife. Henry chides her:

> Remember the country and the age in which we live. Remember that we are English, that we are Christians. Consult your own understanding, your own sense of the probable.... Does our education prepare us for such atrocities? Do our laws connive at them? Could they be perpetrated without being known, in a country like this, ... where every man is surrounded by a neighbourhood of voluntary spies, and where roads and newspapers lay everything open?[3]

---

3. Jane Austen, *Northanger Abbey*, eds. Barbara Benedict and Deirdre Le Faye (New York: Cambridge U.P., 2006), 203.

Outlandish cruelty doesn't happen here. Soon General Tilney, who had credited a rumor that Catherine was an heiress, learns through the same channels that she is merely the daughter of a clergyman. No longer desiring her as a daughter-in-law, he turns her out of his house and denies her even his carriage, so that she must find her own way home—a situation almost as perilous for a young lady as it is insulting. Henry is forbidden to marry Catherine (only to be permitted after all in the final chapter, thanks to a labored stroke of luck).

In Henry's moral, Gothic tropes aren't real. The tapestry conceals no skeleton, and the Tilney family has no dark understory. Here in England is only what meets the eye: the respectable, the probable. In the corrected moral, Gothic horror is a metaphor for English life. Social conventions mystify the operations of power and greed and cruelty, and meritorious persons are not wrong to cultivate a little paranoia. The corrected moral is a bit schematic, a sign of the author's youth, but it helpfully exposes a premise of Austen's mature novels: The social world is darker than it looks.

The "sensitive and penetrating individual" sees the hateful truth concealed by social convention. So argues D. W. Harding in "Regulated Hatred," his seminal essay on Austen, which appeared in F. R. Leavis's *Scrutiny* in 1940.[4] Harding was a war psychologist who thought that people were evil, stupid, and a danger to one another. Social

---

4. D. W. Harding, *Regulated Hatred and Other Essays on Jane Austen* (Atlantic Highlands: Athlone Press, 1998), 160.

convention helped everyone to stay "on reasonably good terms" despite their natural depravity—and thank heaven.[5] But a consequence of this settlement was that detestable people could pass as ordinary, polite, prestigious. *In the country and the age in which we live, could flagrant evil pass unnoticed? Is it probable?* It transpires that Henry's father is both the incarnation of English respectability and a monster of Gothic cruelty.

In her moment of exile, Catherine is an exemplary heroine: The portionless young lady, victim of the tyrant (that is, of society), must make her way in the world. She is a member of the lesser gentry, possessing manners and breeding but no fortune. If a man of means does not rescue her, her exile will be permanent, and she will become a charity case or a governess or worse. Such is the situation of most of Austen's heroines, but especially of those in her first published novel.

II

That novel, *Sense and Sensibility* (1811), has been little loved. It is dark in its portrayal of the social order as a conspiracy of the mediocre against the meritorious, and in its proffer of suitors among whom there is little to choose, since all seem listless or vicious or both. The deficiencies of the men make *Sense and Sensibility* a problem novel, one that leaves us uncertain how to feel about the fortunes it disburses at its close.

---

5. Harding, *Regulated Hatred*, 11-12.

The perils besetting the Dashwood sisters Elinor and Marianne arise from causes natural and social: the deaths of men, and the system of primogeniture. The novel opens with an account of inheritance matters concerning Norland Park, the Dashwood estate in Sussex. The strict settlement of the estate on male heirs leaves the widow and three daughters of the late Mr. Henry Dashwood with no right to continue in their home, and with only £1,000 apiece. It is a daunting beginning—a thicket of legal banalities from which "the family" emerges as a bureaucratic mechanism for consolidating property to the disadvantage of women, and a welter of nephews and great-nephews and great-great-nephews and former and present marriages inducing readers to cry out for a family tree or a flow chart. Then comes a dialogue between the fortunate heir and his wife, who have the power to improve the portions of the widow Dashwood and her daughters. But surely the ladies require only the interest they will receive on their inheritances—"what on earth can four women want for more than that?"[6] A great deal, as it happens. But between the dead hand of primogeniture and the selfishness of the living, the Dashwood ladies can expect very little.

They descend from the landed gentry into the ranks of what might be called the genteel precariat: those (whether dependent ladies or professional men and their families) who have the manners of the landed gentry, and may boast social or familial connections with it, but whose income,

6. Jane Austen, *Sense and Sensibility*, ed. Edward Copeland (New York: Cambridge U.P., 2006), 14.

derived from a profession or from modest investment, is meager or chancy. "Gentility," understood as deportment and connections, is all the more important as their sole claim to inclusion in the only class for which they are fitted. But gentility costs money. The Dashwood ladies calculate that on their £500 of annual income they can afford two maids and a manservant. It is a narrow margin, on the other side of which lie debt and disgrace. They cannot work for money, being ladies, but the girls may hope to make good marriages—a prospect that remains plausible while they maintain their gentility, their "accomplishments," their tastes and talents. Elinor and Marianne are indeed accomplished to a high degree, in an evocation of the superiority they carry (at least Marianne thinks they do) over against a world of intellectual and spiritual nullities.

Mediocrity is exemplified by Sir John and Lady Middleton. Sir John, a distant cousin of Mrs. Dashwood, is by no means a bad fellow. He offers the ladies the cottage in Barton Park on favorable terms just when they need it, and he asks in return only that they socialize on command. They will earn their keep by keeping company. The trouble is with the Middletons' "total want of talent and taste," which makes constant company, none too discerningly selected, "necessary to the happiness of both."[7] As their hospitality is necessitated by their vapidity, their vapidity makes their hospitality a punishment. Sir John's notion of "intimacy" is a few people "sitting an hour or two

---

7. Austen, *Sense and Sensibility*, 38.

together in the same room almost every day"; Lady Middleton distrusts the Dashwood girls "because they [are] fond of reading."[8] With the arrival of Lucy Steele, an able suck-up who is secretly engaged to the man Elinor hopes to marry, odium compounds tedium. The Dashwood girls are stuck in the scenario Harding described: In order to survive, they must regulate their hatred, which entails pretending they can't see that everyone around them is a fool. Marianne resents the obligation keenly and mounts frequent rebellions. "Your Ladyship will have the goodness to excuse *me*—you know I detest cards. I shall go to the piano-forte," and so on.[9] Elinor is constantly on mop-up duty.

It is a commonplace of Austen studies that she created two kinds of heroines: heroines who are right and heroines who are wrong. *Sense and Sensibility* appears to feature one of each. Marianne is "wrong." Her lively talents and aesthetic responsiveness partake of her cultivation of "sensibility," amounting to an ecstatic affinity with either daisies or dead leaves, mood depending. She disdains the dullness of Elinor's beloved, Edward Ferrars, and thinks him unworthy of her sister. Her attachment to her own beloved, the dashing Willoughby, exacerbates her spirited arrogance. As a pair of noble souls—duets on the piano-forte and parlor readings of *Hamlet*—they are entitled, she thinks, to defy convention. Marianne's failure to regulate her adoration leads to a disastrous jilting and a putrid fever that nearly ends in death.

---

8. Austen, *Sense and Sensibility*, 143, 280.

9. Austen, *Sense and Sensibility*, 165.

Her superciliousness chastened by suffering, Marianne comes to praise Elinor as the heroine who is right. Paragon of "sense," Elinor exhibits patience and propriety and politeness. Consider the case of Mrs. Jennings. This wealthy and cheerful but vulgar and silly widow, who hosts the girls in London, elicits the "ungrateful contempt" of Marianne and the amused condescension of readers, above all with her nosy and indelicate joking about the girls' love lives.[10] Harding compares the technique of caricature to the "attitude that we adopt in real life towards someone who is drunk, very ignorant, irritable with tiredness, or in some other way less than an equal companion."[11] We are licensed to regard such characters as lacking full social and moral capacities, as less than fully human. Or are we? Mrs. Jennings becomes more human as we come to know her better. When she commiserates with Marianne over Willoughby's engagement, then "walk[s] on tiptoe out of the room, as if she supposed her young friend's affliction could be increased by noise," we note that foolishness and morally credible goodwill can go together.[12] The moral seems to be, contra Harding, that the meritorious do not regulate their hatred; like Elinor, they abstain from it altogether.

Strikingly, Colonel Brandon dissents. Late-thirties and a wearer of flannel waistcoats, this stolid suitor and "sensible man" values Marianne for her contempt of the

---

10. Austen, *Sense and Sensibility*, 392.

11. Harding, *Regulated Hatred*, 91.

12. Austen, *Sense and Sensibility*, 219.

world, a world of which he has seen too much.[13] When Elinor wishes upon her sister greater "propriety" and "a better acquaintance with the world," Brandon cries, "No, no, do not desire it." He values "the romantic refinements of a young mind" above the "common" opinions that are likely to succeed them.[14]

Is Elinor "right"? Her fond illusions about Edward Ferrars suggest she is fallible. Marianne, of course, has been wrong about Willoughby. His participation in her hackneyed performances of sensibility did not bespeak nobility of soul. At best, Willoughby is an aimless heir whiling away the interval to his inheritance by trifling with women; at worst, he is a predatory lecher. But Elinor is hardly less deceived about her beloved. From the first, Edward is notable for "want of spirits," which seems tied to his evasiveness and reserve.[15] When he appears wearing a ring that bears a lady's plaited hair, Elinor is certain that the hair is hers—despite the fact that she never gave it to him. He must have raided her hairbrush or bribed her maid. Only she, of all English women, has dark hair. This is a self-deception more convoluted than Marianne's refusal to accept the testimony of her senses when Willoughby turns up in London engaged to a Miss Grey.

Elinor's sense cannot keep her from nonsense. It might even be redescribed as a refusal to perceive the badness of the society in which she is sinking, a society in

---

13. Austen, *Sense and Sensibility*, 60.

14. Austen, *Sense and Sensibility*, 66-67.

15. Austen, *Sense and Sensibility*, 25.

which the name of the game is "inheritance, power, and control (mixed in with however much boredom and obsequiousness)."[16] For her generous assessments of Edward partake of the fashion for praising mediocrity as excellence when it appears in those with money. Edward is an unambitious nullity—which, in this novel, is as much as to say he is an elder son. Waiting for his mother to settle money on him, he declines to embark on a career in politics. His preference for the church a mere velleity, he drifts like Willoughby, but without Willoughby's charm. Elinor defends him against Marianne: "I assure you he is by no means deficient in natural taste, though he has not had opportunities of improving it. Had he ever been in the way of learning, I think he would have drawn very well."[17] If this statement is not false, that's only because it is not falsifiable. In the matter of Lucy Steele, Elinor ties herself in knots, pitying rather than blaming Edward for the situation in which he has landed all three of them. Edward is "a second Willoughby" in possessing the vices encouraged by primogeniture, which include the disposition to create expectation and dependence in multiple women.[18]

Though he lacks Willoughby's viciousness, his moral lethargy causes nearly as much mischief. John Wiltshire

16. Margaret Anne Doody, "Introduction," *Sense and Sensibility*, ed. James Kinsley, 3rd ed. (New York: Oxford U.P., 2004), vii-xxxix, xxxix.

17. Austen, *Sense and Sensibility*, 22.

18. Austen, *Sense and Sensibility*, 296.

aptly compares Edward's ring to "an amulet or charm"[19]: Armed with this token of his intended, he travels to Barton, where he intends to keep aloof from Elinor even as he trifles with her. As he tells her later, "the consciousness of my engagement was to keep my heart as safe and sacred as my honour."[20] Edward's "honour" stipulated his commitment to Lucy, that transparent opportunist "whom he had long ceased to love."[21] (In other Austen novels, morally intelligent characters take it for granted that engagements may be broken for a good enough reason, such as lack of affection or the intrinsic dubiousness of secret engagements.[22]) "Honour" curiously did not forbid his making a

---

19. John Wiltshire, *Jane Austen and the Body: "The picture of health"* (New York: Cambridge U.P., 1992), 33.

20. Austen, *Sense and Sensibility*, 417.

21. Austen, *Sense and Sensibility*, 410.

22. In *Pride and Prejudice*, Jane Bennet second-guesses Elizabeth's just-secured engagement to Mr. Darcy: "do anything rather than marry without affection." (We recall that in 1802, Jane Austen accepted a marriage proposal one evening and rejected it the next morning.) In *Emma*, Jane Fairfax breaks off her secret engagement to Frank Churchill, an act presented as morally justified. In scenes of fatherly advice in both *Pride and Prejudice* and *Mansfield Park*, daughters are assured that they need not marry the men they have accepted. Of course, when a man considers throwing over a woman, chivalry imposes a heavier burden. In *Persuasion*, Wentworth judges himself bound to Louisa Musgrove, even without a formal engagement, because she is a nice (and now disabled) girl whose head he injured in the course of courting her, and

special journey over bad roads to amuse himself with the woman he was resolved to disappoint. Not only commitment to Lucy, but also resolution against the woman who truly loved him, are what the mysterious ring betokened.

To Edward's claim that he was "doing no injury to anybody but [him]self," Elinor merely "smiled, and shook her head."[23] She justifies the stern assessment of Margaret Anne Doody: "Edward Ferrars often acts the part of an abject liar and a cad—he is so very miserable, so undashing in the process, however, that he always wins Elinor's prejudiced and protective forgiveness."[24] Elinor's love for Edward seems more maternal than erotic, as though she were filling in for his cold and arbitrary mother, who is busy filling in for his dead father, wielding the patriarch's prerogative to bequeath money or withhold it, to assign and reassign the office of elder son. Family roles can slide around when, as in this novel, they are defined by proximity to power. Mrs. Ferrars is corrupted by the system; Edward opts out. As in any clean-hands scenario, Edward presents less to condemn than do the powerful, but scarcely more to admire. In the comparison with Willoughby, what we may

---

whom he just doesn't happen to love. As will be discussed, Mr. Bennet suggests the scenario in which the meritorious man or woman must break off an engagement: The morally vitiating condition of being "unable to respect your partner in life" is to be avoided at all costs. Jane Austen, *Pride and Prejudice*, ed. Pat Rogers (New York: Cambridge U.P., 2006), 414, 418.

23. Austen, *Sense and Sensibility*, 417.

24. Doody, "Introduction," xxxi.

say for him is that he sires no bastards, and he does marry his Dashwood in the end. But we should not imagine that this feckless gent is a great match for Elinor, or that their domestic life on a modest clerical living bestowed by Brandon constitutes a rectification of the social order that has been arrayed against the Dashwood ladies since their exile.

We arrive at the matter of the unequal marriage—a situation that will be described eloquently in Austen's next novel as the very worst this bad world has to offer. Traditionally, Marianne's marriage to the flannel-clad Brandon has been thought unsatisfactory: Marvin Mudrick protests that "Marianne, the life and centre of the novel, has been betrayed; and not by Willoughby."[25] When a match is a mismatch, it complicates our desire to read the novel as a comedy. We expect marriage to elevate our heroines as they deserve. But in *Sense and Sensibility*, this may be to misunderstand the heroines' relation to their world. No marriage can salvage this world—at least, no marriage this world would ever permit. With reference to the retired life of the Brandons, Claudia Johnson observes that at least Marianne "is never obliged to surrender to the 'commonplace,' 'gross,' and 'illiberal,' and in permitting her to withdraw from the world, *Sense and Sensibility* grants her the highest happiness it can imagine."[26] If secession is the idea, then Brandon is the man.

---

25. Marvin Mudrick, *Jane Austen: Irony as Defense and Discovery* (Berkeley: University of California Press, 1968), 93.

26. Claudia L. Johnson, *Jane Austen: Women, Politics, and the Novel* (Chicago: U. Chicago Press, 1988), 72.

Elinor has abstained from Marianne's countercultural polemics, yet our high valuation of her is inextricable from a low valuation of the society in which she moves. We admire Elinor for her moral discrimination and goodwill, and of course for her "sense," by which she steers her family through rough waters. To praise Elinor for her survival skills is both to indict society (calling attention to the adversity and injustice under which she operates) and to reconcile ourselves to it (accepting these conditions as survivable, and as the staging-ground of her virtues). Her skills include a faculty of realistic appraisal: The Dashwood ladies cannot afford to rent the houses her mother has her eye on; they cannot afford to alienate their benefactors. Elinor is not Lucy—there is calculation, and there is *calculation*. But Lucy is a degraded instance of the same feminine character, a character shaped by social and financial vulnerability. In their tense encounters, Elinor and Lucy contest the degree to which *calculation* should prevail: *So do you love Edward*, Elinor tacitly inquires, *or just want to marry above your station?* Charlotte Lucas of *Pride and Prejudice* is another "sensible, intelligent young woman" noted for realistic appraisals, which in her case extend to a conception of marriage so prudent it is almost impious.[27] Allowances are made, as she is plain and twenty-seven, but we must ask whether Charlotte expects too little and rates herself too low—a question provoked by her ready acceptance of a man with whom she should be more dissatisfied than she is. If *calculation* encourages aspiration

27. Austen, *Pride and Prejudice*, 19.

above one's station, calculation may encourage self-deception as to the acceptability of inferior products. Elinor's case is more discomfiting than Charlotte's because she commands greater admiration for her merit and occupies the role of heroine. Her sense, no less than her nonsense, inclines her to rationalize conditions that should raise a protest.

Moreover, there is an odd thing about asymmetrical matches: "She deserves better" is said of *her* to the detriment of *him*, but what are we to think of *her* if she thinks the match symmetrical—if she does not share our conviction of her superiority to him? Elinor believes that Edward abundantly deserves her, a striking opinion in a novel that stresses the necessity of sorting the meritorious from the mediocre. Brandon, though scarcely more dashing than Edward, is at least forthright and honorable. If Austen betrayed Marianne, Elinor betrayed herself. A darker thought than "She deserves better" is "Then again, maybe she doesn't."

III

It is worth asking why Austen would do something so apparently perverse as write a comedy that ends with marriages that might not be happy. Why defy generic expectations, inviting reader dissatisfaction (of just the sort that *Sense and Sensibility* has long provoked)? I can only hazard that Austen is expressing moral dissatisfaction: The mediocracy captures just about everyone, even the heroine who is "right." This state of affairs offends the Austen who is dedicated to "kicking sin, cuffing stupidity, ridiculing the vulgar and cruel—and assigning sovereign power to tenderness, talent and pride" (this is Vladimir Nabokov talking about himself, but it serves).[28] If the mediocracy does not capture the heroine who is "wrong," if Brandon is the surprising means by which Marianne is to maintain her independence, then to that extent the darkness is cabined. But this is simply to recapitulate the questioning of rightness and wrongness. The heroine who is "right" earns her title by making do in a social order that systematically crushes merit. If Marianne's rebellion cannot succeed except in a small way and through the condescension of a burnt-out case like Brandon, such an outcome is—again—dark. The social order begrudges any accommodation of tenderness, talent, and pride.

One purpose of marriage is to secure such an accommodation. Of its nature, marriage is both an integration and a defection. It links the couple with other households and makes them a link in the chain of generation. It also permits the spouses' loyalty to each other before all else and their belief in each other's primacy over all the world. Married lovers "assuage their loneliness without paying the price of full conformity," writes Harding, hence the centrality of marriage to "the survival of the sensitive and penetrating individual in a society of conforming

---

28. Vladimir Nabokov, *Strong Opinions*, 2nd ed. (New York: Vintage International, 1990), 193.

mediocrity."[29] The equal marriage, uniting two worthy people who deserve each other, is thus the very type of felicity in Austen's novels. The unequal marriage, the condition of being "unable to respect your partner in life," is the very type of misery, leading to demoralization and moral decay.[30] The equal marriage rewards merit, the unequal marriage punishes it.

The theorist of the unequal marriage is Mr. Bennet of *Pride and Prejudice*, Austen's commercial breakthrough, published two years after *Sense and Sensibility*. One of the mysteries of English literature is how old Austen was when she composed *Pride and Prejudice*. It had its beginnings in epistolary juvenilia, long lost; as to how drastic the revisions were, and when they were completed, theories vary widely. It seems safe to say that it must have been some years before the book's 1813 publication, and that she must have been in her twenties, because the technical and thematic distance between the artistic period culminating in *Pride and Prejudice* and the so-called Chawton novels is considerable. The latter were written during the Austen ladies' residence at Chawton in Hampshire, which began in 1809. They show a gain in formal complexity and sophistication over *Pride and Prejudice*, as though with that novel she had exhausted the possibilities of lapidary narration and set-piece repartee. They also exhibit a shift of tone and emphasis, which we are tempted to

---

29. Harding, *Regulated Hatred*, 159-60.

30. Austen, *Pride and Prejudice*, 418.

read biographically: ever more urgent representations of social change, social precarity, physical frailty, and death. Delaying our discussion of the novel that Austen famously deprecated as "too light, and bright, and sparkling," too deficient in "shade," we turn now to the first of the Chawton novels.[31]

IV

There is ample shade in *Mansfield Park* (1814), in which the great house of the title is anything but. Another problem novel, more caustic than comic, *Mansfield Park* concludes in a marriage we are not sure we can approve, between a heroine we are not sure we like and a hero who does not impress. The stakes of critique seem higher in this novel than in *Sense and Sensibility*. Here, a sustained focus on the inner life of a landed estate suggests an indictment of great-house conservatism, a major ideology of social concord in Austen's age. The atmosphere at Mansfield is claustral; imagery of illness and imprisonment is rife. The corruption of the great house is the worst.

Mansfield is the hereditary estate of Sir Thomas Bertram. His inert wife hails from the lesser gentry but, as the beautiful Miss Maria Ward, made a brilliant marriage to a baronet. Her two sisters married laterally (to a

31. Jane Austen to Cassandra Austen, Feb. 4, 1813, in *The Letters of Jane Austen*, ed. Sarah Chauncey Woolsey (Boston: Little, Brown, 1908), 183.

clergyman named Norris) and down (to a drunken sergeant of marines named Price). The latter union produced our heroine, Fanny. Reared among the Bertram children at Mansfield but instructed that she does not belong, Fanny possesses a vivid moral sense, which becomes her compass when the Crawford siblings, full of metropolitan charm, come to visit.

They enter a house of sickness and decay. The motif encompasses the dissipation and physical crisis of Tom, the Bertram heir; the wear-and-tear evident on Sir Thomas's person upon his return from travel; and Fanny's headaches and dizzy spells, which are difficult to separate from her youthful "bloom," which elicits her discomposure and hypochondria whenever it obtrudes. "Healthy growth" and "healthy eroticism," clichés outside this novel, are oxymorons where Fanny is concerned.

We thus approach her controversial status as a heroine who is "right." Twentieth-century critics recoiled from her; Harding calls her "a dreary, debilitated, priggish goody-goody," and Lionel Trilling declares that "Nobody … has ever found it possible to like the heroine of *Mansfield Park*."[32] In Whit Stillman's film *Metropolitan* (1990), Audrey Rouget speaks for the defense: "What's wrong with a novel having a virtuous heroine?"[33] Of course

---

32. Harding, *Regulated Hatred*, 121-22; Lionel Trilling, "Mansfield Park," in *The Moral Obligation To Be Intelligent*, ed. Leon Wieseltier, 2nd ed. (Chicago: Northwestern U.P., 2008), 292-310, 296.

33. *Metropolitan*, dir. Whit Stillman (1990; New York: Criterion Collection, 2012), Blu-ray.

nothing is wrong with it. One problem in Fanny's case is that her morality is slave morality. Her accent on denial and constraint is not extricable from her self-image as a nobody who deserves nothing, the constant message of her Aunt Norris. As libido is inconsistent with self-effacement, we have a key to her anxiety about sex. More public is Fanny's preference for "domestic tranquillity," which is inconsistent with the perturbations introduced by private theatricals, the curious scandal on which the first volume pivots.[34] She is at one with Sir Thomas. He is away, tending to financial interests in Antigua, but everyone understands that he would forbid the performance of Kotzebue's *Lovers' Vows* under his roof. He returns from Antigua hymning "a home which shuts out noisy pleasures."[35] William Deresiewicz glosses "the Mansfield ideal" as "a purely negative one of happiness as that which causes no 'agitation' or 'vexation' or 'trouble.'"[36] Fanny tracks the patriarch's principles very accurately.

As for us, we may resent the presentation of peace and quiet as a moral imperative, and doubt whether the lighthearted Crawfords really are the problem. It is open to us to judge that Fanny does not always judge aright. She values things dear and near—things that may in reality be pretty shabby, and often are agents or instruments of

---

34. Jane Austen, *Mansfield Park*, ed. John Wiltshire (New York: Cambridge U.P., 2005), 218.

35. Austen, *Mansfield Park*, 218.

36. William Deresiewicz, *Jane Austen and the Romantic Poets* (New York: Columbia U.P., 2004), 69-70.

her oppression. She "comes too near relishing the role of being downtrodden," and "like a grateful slave she lets particular and small acts of kindness overshadow" the larger truth of her subjugation.[37] Her cousin Edmund, whom she admires and desires, is "an example of everything good and great."[38] The very name of Edmund is "a name of heroism and renown; of kings, princes, and knights; and seems to breathe the spirit of chivalry and warm affections."[39] Since Fanny's arrival at Mansfield, Edmund has earned her gratitude by attending to her feelings, however belatedly in some instances. But often he aims in his solicitude to reconcile her to hardship when he might better relieve her. In his uncertain interest in Mary Crawford, he exhibits discomfort with women's freedom of thought and speech. Fanny, of course, outpaces him in her objections to Mary's "lively mind."[40]

If Fanny is the exponent of Mansfield principles, then she would seem to occupy prestigious territory at the moral center of the novel. Indeed, the question "Who deserves to live in the great house?" is often a way of asking which characters in an Austen novel possess the greatest merit, the truest morality. We feel that Elinor and Marianne have a better right to Norland Park than do the greedy mediocrities who supplant them. Notably, the question is never

---

37. Harding, *Regulated Hatred*, 193; Johnson, *Austen*, 108.

38. Austen, *Mansfield Park*, 43.

39. Austen, *Mansfield Park*, 246.

40. Austen, *Mansfield Park*, 75.

"Who deserves a noble title?" Austen was no respecter of titles. She was a respecter, at least potentially, of landed wealth, which brought responsibility and revealed the proprietor's character according as he lived up to it (or didn't).

Mansfield Park is Austen's great-house novel par excellence, featuring two country houses in addition to the titular one. But the houses and their proprietors are deficient. Mansfield is dreary. Architecturally and historically undistinguished, it attracts no sightseers, unlike nearby Sotherton. It is physically remote, surrounded by bad roads in the Northamptonshire countryside. It is socially isolated, having little commerce with the village. No dinners are exchanged except with the parsonage in the park. No wonder the Bertram girls, Maria and Julia, long for a house in town for the social season. Rebellion is brewing. Maria quotes Laurence Sterne: "I cannot get out, as the starling said."[41] In the moral-political ideal enunciated by Edmund Burke, liberty and happiness were best secured by patriarchal stricture. But the Bertram girls experience Sir Thomas's authority as mere "restraint and hardship."[42] Ever since Edward Said's *Culture and Imperialism* opened with a chapter on Austen, academia has viewed Sir Thomas's investment in the sugar trade as the dark heart of *Mansfield Park*, and the ladies in his family as analogously enslaved. A parallel between English women and African slaves was a staple of the feminist hyperbole

---

41. Austen, *Mansfield Park*, 116.

42. Austen, *Mansfield Park*, 116.

of Mary Wollstonecraft and Hannah More, and Austen appears to evoke it when presenting Fanny's blindness to the injustice of her own position.[43] But the novel's major metaphor for domestic oppression is not enslavement but imprisonment.

If Mansfield is a prison, Sotherton, which dates from "Elizabeth's time," is a heritage site, and one not intelligently curated.[44] Its owner is Mr. Rushworth. Fanny, the novel's great-house ideologue, is distressed by his talk of felling oaks and other "improvements" that will wreck the property's historic and aesthetic significance. She decries the disuse into which the chapel has fallen: "There is something in a chapel and chaplain so much in character with a great house, with one's ideas of what such a household should be!"[45] One need not concur in Fanny's ideals to deplore Rushworth's insensibility to them.

Mr. Rushworth is engaged to Maria Bertram, as Sir Thomas discovers upon his return from Antigua. A tense conference between father and daughter establishes that, whatever else is true, Sir Thomas is not auctioning the Bertram ladies to the highest bidder, as the postcolonial critics would have it. He tries to dissuade Maria from marrying a man who has nothing to recommend him except £12,000 per annum (princely, in fairness) and a house in town. Rushworth is what Mr. Bennet feared Mr. Darcy was, but

43. John Wiltshire, "Decolonising *Mansfield Park*," *Essays in Criticism* 53.4 (2003): 303-22, 308.

44. Austen, *Mansfield Park*, 66.

45. Austen, *Mansfield Park*, 101.

whereas Elizabeth was able to speak feelingly of the merits of her intended, Maria despises hers. Yet she avows that Rushworth is her choice, and Sir Thomas suppresses his misgivings. *Mansfield Park* thus depicts a grave lack of insight and rapport among daughter, father, and suitor. If the houses are not great in this novel, neither are the men.

Henry Crawford's estate is Everingham, which we never visit and neither, it seems, does he. From his remarks we gather that he has little to do with its management but would be open to some of those notorious "improvements." Accordingly, when he determines to marry Fanny and receives the backing of the Mansfield men, she is horrified. Refusing Henry, against the patriarchal sublimity of Sir Thomas and the moralistic suasions of Edmund, is Fanny's great stand—calling Mansfield back to its principles, against Crawfordism.

But what if the Crawfords aren't so bad? Along with excitement, variance, and pleasure, they bring to Mansfield indignation over the deprivations and humiliations to which Fanny is subject: "dependent, helpless, friendless, neglected, forgotten," in Henry's words.[46] During rehearsals for *Lovers' Vows*, when Mrs. Norris admonishes Fanny in front of everyone to remember "who and what she is," Mary, shocked, scoots her chair next to Fanny's and becomes her comrade for the evening, in a show of fellow-feeling that no Bertram, including Edmund, ever equals.[47] But Fanny prefers Mansfield pure. "I was

---

46. Austen, *Mansfield Park*, 344.

47. Austen, *Mansfield Park*, 173.

quiet, but I was not blind": Her oft-quoted assertion of moral agency expresses her disapproval of Henry's early flirtation with the affianced Maria, a blamable escapade to be sure.[48] But we note that her blame falls heavily on the Crawford brother and lightly on the Bertram daughter; she criticizes Mansfield only in its susceptibility to the Crawfords. In the end, Maria will abandon Rushworth to abscond with Henry, apparently justifying Fanny's rejection of him. But we have the narrator's word that Maria was the active agent: A Bertram seduced a Crawford. Worse, had Henry resisted Maria and "persevered" with Fanny, she "must have been his reward—and a reward very voluntarily bestowed."[49] There was, after all, nothing morally or even psychologically necessary in Fanny's great refusal.

Of course, they shouldn't twist her arm. Sir Thomas is at his very worst when calling his niece ungrateful and rebellious because she wants to have a say in whom she marries. But her better idea is—what now?

Cousin-marriage was by no means unheard of in Austen's England, especially in dynastic families with property and prestige to consolidate. In *Pride and Prejudice*, Darcy and his cousin Anne have been "intended" for each other from the cradle. In their case, we understand what we are to think: The match is a nonstarter not only because there is no eros between the cousins, but because the lady is an emblem of lineal exhaustion. "Sickly and

---

48. Austen, *Mansfield Park*, 419.
49. Austen, *Mansfield Park*, 540.

cross" and a suspected mute, she surely cannot procreate.[50] The consolidated lines would shortly go extinct, in a damning comment on Darcy's training to "think meanly" of everyone outside his family circle.[51] In the end, in his elevation of a spirited woman from the genteel precariat, he is rewarded for impulses not just egalitarian but exogamous.

In *Mansfield Park* the presentation of cousin-marriage is more ambiguous. The prospect is made akin to sibling incest by Fanny's rearing in Edmund's father's house; an early discussion between Sir Thomas and Mrs. Norris declares it unthinkable for this reason. (Relevant here is Fanny's intense attachment to her brother William, with whom she shares a "tie" above "the conjugal," and the siblings' dream of living out their golden years in a cottage he will purchase with his navy earnings.)[52] Marriage to her brotherly cousin is our heroine's heart's desire, and when the novelist gives it to her in "a perfunctorily adopted anticlimax," we may feel pressure to regard it as a reward for good behavior, even if it is too close for comfort.[53] But "comfort" is the keyword of the novel's end; it occurs fourteen times in the final chapter. Fanny becomes the "prime comfort" of Sir Thomas in part because, after approving the suits of Rushworth and Crawford, he is regretting his attempts to have commerce with the world.[54] "Domestic

---

50. Austen, *Pride and Prejudice*, 180.

51. Austen, *Pride and Prejudice*, 409.

52. Austen, *Mansfield Park*, 273.

53. Johnson, *Austen*, 114.

54. Austen, *Mansfield Park*, 546.

tranquillity," untroubled by strangers, secured by endogamous marriage, will "[deaden] his sense of what was lost."[55]

Is Fanny a heroine who is right? Does she marry well? She may be less a moral lodestar than an A-student with a merit scholarship, hitting the books while the prep-school kids do cocaine, a true believer in the "ideals" of a system whose corruption it is not in her interest to perceive. She wins only booby-prizes: honor within a dark house full of vitiated figures, marriage to a man who favors what is tame and spiritless. At least it may be said that the cousins deserve each other.

Mrs. Norris, who set up the Rushworth marriage, partakes of Maria's disgrace. A sinister caricature, she usually takes the laurel for the most odious character in Austen. Harding writes that "the technique of caricature allows Jane Austen to express ... astonishment at the way the most outrageously deformed personalities are allowed [a] part in society."[56] Readers perceive Mrs. Norris as outrageous, but the Bertrams, as a rule, do not. Enforcing hierarchy and scarcity economics, she has been integral to the moral and practical operations of Mansfield. Her "removal" at the end is purgative. And yet, "Something must have been wanting *within*": Sir Thomas sees that Mrs. Norris is "part of himself," that her acts have been effects of his will, of his

---

55. Austen, *Mansfield Park*, 536.

56. Harding, *Regulated Hatred*, 101.

own "grievous mismanagement."[57] If there are grounds for hope in *Mansfield Park*, they are these: Sir Thomas has confronted darkness and acknowledged it within.

V

Though not deficient in shade, *Emma* (1815) is sunnier than *Mansfield Park*. From its first sentence, it is set apart from earlier novels: Its heroine is by no means portionless. "Handsome, clever, and rich," Emma Woodhouse does not await a husband to elevate her.[58]

"Fortune I do not want; . . . consequence I do not want," and she believes that "few married women are half as much mistress of their husband's house" as she is of her father's.[59] Her life already perfect, in what kind of story can she be a heroine?

Emma's is partly a story of moral education, as she learns to regulate her hatred of social inferiors and spiritual superiors. It is partly the story of her susceptibility, after all, to natural and social evils. She is not proof against loneliness or social precarity or the difficulty of knowing other people's hearts and her own. And there is the final

---

57. Austen, *Mansfield Park*, 538, 535.

58. Jane Austen, *Emma*, eds. Richard Cronin and Dorothy McMillan (New York: Cambridge U.P., 2005), 3.

59. Austen, *Emma*, 90-91.

change—death—which shadows the village of Highbury and claims its tribute many times over.

Emma is often called an idyll. Highbury is detailed in every rung of its hierarchy, which extends from its benevolent elite (Mr. Knightley of Donwell Abbey, Mr. and Miss Woodhouse of Hartfield) down through a semi-genteel professional class and declining gentry to shop-keepers and tenant-farmers and the poor cottagers whose names Emma knows, whom she visits when they fall ill. Like Emma in her self-conception, Highbury gives an impression of arcadian self-sufficiency. People circulate socially, goods circulate charitably. Everyone and everything is taken care of; nothing is needed and nothing need change. *Emma* is the only Austen novel in which the scene never shifts.

But the scene is shifting itself. London, only sixteen miles away, is fast expanding, turning villages into suburbs. And Highbury is in vertical motion: If it was once a happening place, its "brilliant days ha[ve] long passed away."[60] As for its professionals and tradesmen, they cannot be called a precariat, because they do nothing but rise. The apothecary will soon set up a carriage. The vicar, who does not hail from "the best society," marries the socially aggressive heiress of a fortune made in the Bristol slave-trade.[61] The Coles ("in trade, and only moderately genteel") have the presumption to begin hosting balls and

---

60. Austen, *Emma*, 213.

61. Austen, *Emma*, 146.

the effrontery to consider not inviting Miss Woodhouse.[62] When all the social energy is among the pseudo-gentry, the traditional gentry may feel or fear a loss of stature.

Other traditional elites have completed their descensions. Miss Bates is the central case in Harding's "Regulated Hatred": A "woman neither young, handsome, rich, nor married," she has "no intellectual superiority to make atonement to herself, or frighten those who might hate her into outward respect."[63] Emma, an imperfectly regulated hater, expresses contempt for old maids with narrow incomes; in the famous scene on Box Hill, she will scorn Miss Bates openly. Like Austen the unmarried daughter of a deceased vicar, but unlike Austen lacking brothers with money, Miss Bates lives with her mother in poverty relieved by apples from Donwell and meat from Hartfield. She is notorious for her loquacity. Her conversation is full of apple-dumplings, and the rivets of broken spectacles, and kitchen chimneys, and asparagus, and soup. She prattles about gifts and favors from her friends, on whose charity she depends: "the beautiful hindquarter of pork you sent us."[64] And she is full of concern for her friends: "Pray take care, Miss Woodhouse, ours is rather a dark staircase—rather darker and narrower than one could wish."[65] She is, as Emma says, "so silly—so satisfied—so smil-

62. Austen, *Emma*, 223.

63. Austen, *Emma*, 20.

64. Austen, *Emma*, 186.

65. Austen, *Emma*, 258.

ing—so prosing—so undistinguishing and unfastidious," that we are tempted to regard her as a caricature, as less than fully human.[66]

Certainly we are tempted to skim her speeches, her monologues masquerading as dialogue. But listen carefully and they convey a great deal of social information. "Ours is rather a dark staircase": This is an apology for her poverty. Her household is poor and getting poorer. Windows are expensive, as are candles. It is also a warning that the world is full of peril. Watch your step—Miss Bates knows what hazards may befall you on your way up or (especially) down. Take John Abdy, who once was clerk to the Reverend Mr. Bates and has since gone down in the world. Bedridden with "the rheumatic gout," requiring relief from the parish, he exists for us only in Miss Bates's mention of him.[67] Her loquacity may be understood as the endless postponement of the final implication of social precarity. She talks around (and therefore persistently suggests) the impolite truth: Poverty can kill. Her niece is Jane Fairfax, a portionless young woman of great elegance and accomplishment. Jane was orphaned by consumption, and now it is feared that she, with her delicate (tubercular) style of beauty, is consumptive herself or will become so, especially if poverty forces her to turn to governessing.

Gossip about Jane's health is one instance of Highbury's preoccupation with sickness and medicine. Mr. Woodhouse, the ranking hypochondriac, sets the tone.

---

66. Austen, *Emma*, 91.

67. Austen, *Emma*, 416.

A "valetudinarian all his life," he is "a much older man in ways than in years."[68] He rarely walks outside; fears open doors and "the dews of a summer evening"[69]; almost gives up the ghost when he has to ride in a coach while snow is falling; idolizes his apothecary; considers wedding-cake unwholesome; and regrets that when he hosts people for supper, he has to inflict food on them—he advises a *small* apple tart, a *small* half-glass of wine, and no custard. He is forever seeking the perfect consistency of gruel: smooth and thin, but not too thin.

Jane gets headaches. Harriet Smith suffers a sore throat, then a toothache. Mr. Perry has bile, Isabella Knightley palpitations, Mrs. Weston a "condition," Frank Churchill a "constitution." Jane, Harriet, Isabella, and Mrs. Weston all have nerves. That Mr. Woodhouse's neurosis should be the fashion in Highbury, more than Mr. Knightley's bluff and salubrious style, is notable. Knightley is an active local elite, Mr. Woodhouse a figurehead. And Knightley, with his ancient landed estate, outranks Mr. Woodhouse, with his "modern" house and liquid assets. But the comparative newness of Hartfield is suggestive. Nervous complaints were a new disorder in the early nineteenth century, "the product of increasing wealth and leisure among the middle classes."[70] Modernity is embodied here by the elderly and atrophied.

---

68. Austen, *Emma*, 5.

69. Austen, *Emma*, 225.

70. Wiltshire, *Austen and the Body*, 117.

The novel's other ailing eminence is the never-seen Mrs. Churchill, whose hypochondria, a more blatant power play than Mr. Woodhouse's, forces the question of the real and the unreal. She is the wealthy aunt of the much-admired Frank Churchill; news of her health emergencies calls him from Highbury repeatedly. "As to her illness, all nothing of course."[71] Mrs. Churchill is constantly dying—therefore not dying at all—until one day she up and dies. All nothing? Since the cause of her death is said to be unrelated to her chronic complaints, there remains a sense in which she really was *not* dying before she died, except in the sense in which we all are.

Like loquacity, hypochondria is a technique of evasion. Mr. Woodhouse, "fond of every body that he was used to, and hating to part with them; hating change of every kind," seeks to suppress appetite and sensation.[72] In the perfect consistency of gruel he seeks the textureless, flavorless, changeless. In wedding-cake he rejects not just gustation but generation. The novel opens on the day Mr. Weston has married "poor Miss Taylor." "Poor" is not exactly the word for a former governess who has just married the third-ranking man of the neighborhood, but "[m]atrimony, as the origin of change, was always disagreeable."[73] Mr. Woodhouse's insight is that all change alludes to death.

Emma does not share her father's hypochondria, yet it threatens her with confinement and stagnation. She

71. Austen, *Emma*, 328.
72. Austen, *Emma*, 6.
73. Austen, *Emma*, 6.

literalizes his presumption that marriage means death: She cannot marry while he lives, since marriage would mean her leaving his household, which would kill him. Her deftness and patience in managing his sensitivities are remarkable in a vivacious girl of twenty, and greatly to her credit; but the task keeps her at home when she should be abroad. Emma never goes to London (at this rate it will come to her before she visits it) and has never seen the sea. Her lofty resolution on celibacy dignifies her commitment to elder-care, but there are indications that she is restless. She is glum when the novel opens, for with the loss of Miss Taylor her family circle has shrunk by one-third. She cannot expect to pay many visits to the newlyweds, as the half-mile distance is too far for the propriety and safety of a lady walking alone, and Mr. Woodhouse discourages use of the carriage, out of consideration for the groom and horses. For all her bustling engagement in and around the village, she is subject to fixity and isolation in her domestic sphere. We may therefore question whether she really possesses such great "resources" as she boasts will make celibacy agreeable.[74] Near the novel's end, thinking that Knightley intends to marry Harriet, she decides that there is no great difference after all between wealthy and poor spinsters, between a Miss Woodhouse and a Miss Bates. Wealth and consequence will not salvage the basic situation: confinement, isolation, absorption in the care of a declining parent—a role-reversal that is common and

74. Austen, *Emma*, 92.

proper, except when it is to the exclusion of generation—and afterwards, no one at all to be "first" with.[75] Emma once averred that "poverty only" made spinsterhood "contemptible."[76] But poverty takes many forms; lack of a husband and children is one.

In the end she avoids it. Invited to return indoors where her father is immured with the apothecary, she instead takes another turn in the shrubbery with Knightley; his profession follows. Emma learns that "Harriet was nothing; that she was every thing herself," and the sudden clarity is like a break in the clouds.[77] Emma has been oppressed by the folly of her famous misreadings: "I seem to have been doomed to blindness."[78] And yet *Emma* evinces a less skeptical social epistemology than do some other Austen novels. Opacity prevailed in *Sense and Sensibility*, even in the most intimate relations: Not only did Elinor and Marianne hardly know their lovers, but the Dashwood ladies hardly knew each other. *Was Marianne engaged to Willoughby?* wondered Elinor and her mother. *Unthinkable to ask.* Emma has found it difficult to know her own heart—it was with a shock that she discovered, none too soon, that "Mr. Knightley must marry no one but herself!"—much less his, despite his long intimacy with her family.[79] The narrator is full of reassurance: "Seldom, very seldom, does

75. Austen, *Emma*, 452.

76. Austen, *Emma*, 91.

77. Austen, *Emma*, 469.

78. Austen, *Emma*, 464.

79. Austen, *Emma*, 444.

complete truth belong to any human disclosure; . . . but where, as in this case, though the conduct is mistaken, the feelings are not, it may not be very material."[80]

As for strangers? "Pray take care, Miss Woodhouse." Emma takes people either too seriously or not seriously enough—is either too credulous of self-presentations (as with the inaptly named Frank) or too skeptical (as with Jane). Her suspicion that Jane is hiding something, and her eager indulgence in gossip about her affairs of the heart, are motivated partly by envy. Emma has long resented and neglected Jane, who is in many ways her superior: more elegant and more accomplished, despite straitened circumstances. "One is sick of the very name of Jane Fairfax," Emma exclaims.[81] In her fantasy of Jane's guilty pining for a Mr. Dixon, she is encouraged by Frank, who knows better than anyone what nonsense it is. "It may not be very material." Then again, it may.

Frank is secretly engaged to Jane—secretly, because his snobbish aunt would disinherit him if she knew. He comes to Highbury to be near Jane but spends much of his energy on a flirtation with Emma, ostensibly a "blind" to divert suspicion from his real attachment. He creates less havoc than he might, because Emma is "somehow or other safe from him"—in love with Knightley, though not yet aware of it.[82] But the charade so distresses Jane as to imperil the engagement. Knightley susses out the whole thing; he also

80. Austen, *Emma*, 470.

81. Austen, *Emma*, 92.

82. Austen, *Emma*, 466.

overestimates Emma's feeling for Frank, and from rational disapproval compounded by jealousy, heartily detests him. When Frank and Jane's engagement becomes public, Knightley predicts that Jane "will be a miserable creature."[83] But when, in the course of a turn in the shrubbery, he learns that Emma loves not Frank but himself, the exigency recedes, and "if he could have thought of Frank Churchill then, he might have deemed him a very good sort of fellow."[84] Critics generally credit Knightley with coming around to the right judgment. But he was right, more right than he knew, the first time.

Frank is an Edward Ferrars who enjoys the game. He plays it with some flair. His worshipful attention to Emma on Box Hill, when Jane is plainly in agony, is quite a flourish. He is not insensible to the moral difficulty of his position, but through luxuriant self-regard he converts guilt to pleasure. Early on, he *almost* confesses to Emma what he's been up to, but runs out of time before he is fetched to the carriage. It would have been easily accomplished had he not sat so long heaving sighs. Of course there are some threadbare lies. When Jane, finally exhausted by her "life of deceit" and demoralized by his attentions to Emma, writes to him breaking off their engagement, he pens a prompt reply to patch things up and,—whoops!—forgets it in his writing-desk, accidentally increasing her

---

83. Austen, *Emma*, 465.
84. Austen, *Emma*, 472.

anguish and driving her to accept a post as a governess.[85] (The truth between the lines: He was not about to let her threaten him with a breakup, and chose to delay his reply in order to show her who was boss. A few days later, alerted to her acceptance of the governess job, he saw that he had pushed his advantage too far.)

The pretext for his blind was never credible, as Jane pleads repeatedly. His aunt is in Richmond and cannot observe his behavior to either lady. He enjoys toying with Emma; he especially enjoys torturing Jane. In one mode of flirtation, he disparages the latter's looks. She is too pale for his taste: "so pale, as almost always to give the appearance of ill health.—A most deplorable want of complexion."[86] At the Coles ball, he finds that she

> "has done her hair in so odd a way—so very odd a way—that I cannot keep my eyes from her. I never saw any thing so outrée!—Those curls!—This must be a fancy of her own. I see nobody else looking like her!—I must go and ask her whether it is an Irish fashion. Shall I?—Yes, I will—I declare I will—and you shall see how she takes it;—whether she colours."[87]

---

85. Austen, *Emma*, 501, 482.

86. Austen, *Emma*, 214.

87. Austen, *Emma*, 240.

His excuse will be that Emma has noticed him sneaking looks at Jane, and by this trick he converts his faux pas into a tête-à-tête. He does it by exposing his fiancée to the ridicule of a woman who resents her, and whom she regards as her romantic rival. The same skin and hair he savaged when Jane was his secret, he boasts in once the secret is out. He sits with Emma a few yards from Jane, anatomizing her beauty, confiding a plan to have "an ornament" made "for the head."[88] No other Austenian "hero" speaks of his intended as though she were a piece of statuary. Frank exhibits a hostile interest in attractive young women—Emma and Jane both, but more so Jane, whose combination of personal superiority and social inferiority makes her both daunting and weak. He brings out the very worst in Emma: not the matchmaker, who after all is well-intentioned, but the occasional hater of what is below her and what is above.

The understory of Frank and Jane is dark enough. Worse is that their neighbors remain cheerfully in the dark. In a widely circulated letter, Frank confesses (seemingly) everything: not just his conduct, but his agitation consequent upon his conduct. A performance of self-laceration, done with feeling, whether genuine or not, must secure forgiveness. Our paladin Knightley relents in his criticism, a little grumpily, rather than mar the happy ending. He backs off "She deserves a better fate" and says instead that Frank is "likely to be happier than he deserves," though

88. Austen, *Emma*, 522-23.

he may improve under Jane's influence.[89] With this permission, most readers look on the bright side. Everything is clarified. "Oh!" cries Emma to Jane, "if you knew how much I love every thing that is decided and open!"[90] But the letter contains lies. Just as Knightley once read between the lines of Frank and Jane's behavior, we now must ask what Frank was and is really up to, what Jane has suffered and will suffer.

Emma calls Frank "the child of good fortune."[91] He will never be held to account by his social circle, that external monitor which does him the office of a conscience (to the extent that anything does). Prying as a rule, but happy to bask in his goldenness, his circle will decide his business is none of theirs as soon as their interest inconveniences him. Highbury was captivated by Jane's walks to the post office when she was struggling to conceal her secret correspondence. No interest is taken in Frank's black hole of a writing-desk. Nor will Jane serve as his conscience; we have seen how readily he ignores her corrections.

It may be thought uncharitable to predict unhappiness for Jane. Who would wish it on her, or wish to think ill of him? But Knightley, the greatest moral intelligence in the novel, never really alters his view of Frank. He "might"— *might*—"have deemed him a very good sort of fellow," *if* he had thought of him in the moment when he ceased to be

89. Austen, *Emma*, 464, 488.

90. Austen, *Emma*, 502.

91. Austen, *Emma*, 483.

envious of him. As it happens, he had better things to think about. Later, he obeys the social imperative, enunciated by Emma, to read Frank's letter "with a kinder spirit towards him"—that is, to regard Frank's badness and Jane's sadness as none of his business. But he is above all eager to drop the subject and take up the pleasant puzzle of where he and his own bride are to live. "I cannot think any longer about Frank Churchill."[92] There are indeed better things to think about.

Society is full of hateful people. But for those who don't notice, it may not be very material.

VI

Emma contains a hint that the economic model of the landed gentry is becoming dated. Knightley holds a distinguished old estate but a small one, and it is unclear how sufficient his rent-roll is. He practices economies, "having little spare money," and he can "ill spare Robert Martin," whose competence as a farmer helps Donwell stay in the black.[93] It seems that Knightley could use an influx of a more modern style of wealth. And indeed his happy ending involves marriage to a woman of less storied but more abundant and more liquid assets—anticipating the cash-for-titles practice that would become notorious later in the century, but in this instance simply a triumph of love and land management.

---

92. Austen, *Emma*, 488.
93. Austen, *Emma*, 230, 516.

If *Emma* shows a landed gentleman maintaining his position in "such days as these," in *Persuasion* this rank of men is exhausted.[94] Their representative is a vain baronet named Sir Walter Elliot, who is too busy annotating his family's entry in the *Baronetage* and applying Gowland's Lotion to his face to manage Kellynch, the ancient Elliot estate, and accordingly must rent out the house to save his finances. Our heroine is his daughter Anne, who deplores her father as "a foolish, spendthrift baronet, who had not had principle or sense enough to maintain himself in the situation in which Providence had placed him."[95] Anne has all the natural feelings of sadness and dislocation upon leaving her home of twenty-seven years. But she produces no ideological lament for the great house, such as we would expect from Fanny Price; she does not in principle deplore its becoming available for lease or purchase. Those who do not steward it do not deserve it. In an index of his unworthiness, Sir Walter does not render his patrimony even the tribute of jealousy, once grand enough accommodations have been procured for him in Bath, and once it is established that the man who will supplant him in Kellynch Hall is a handsome personage. *Persuasion* is a novel about precarity and liquidity, of assets and of social forms, and about the new: A professional meritocracy is rising. This novel's impressive men are naval captains and admirals.

---

94. Austen, *Pride and Prejudice*, 41.

95. Jane Austen, *Persuasion*, eds. Janet Todd and Antje Blank (New York: Cambridge U.P., 2006), 270.

Persuasion's focus on the baronetcy—the titled stratum of the gentry—is apt, because the novel depicts a gentry evacuated of significance. In Austen, titles are empty signifiers, or rather they signify emptiness. Sir Walter illustrates the rule by obsessing over his inherited privilege to the exclusion of the duties that attend it. His tenants are extremely underwhelmed by his leavetaking, so little do they think of him, so little have they seen of him. His estranged heir, the distant cousin William Walter Elliot, takes a more modern view of inherited privilege. But his approach cannot be approved, either. Years ago Mr. Elliot relinquished his claim to the baronetcy in order to marry a "very low" but wealthy woman. "[I]f baronetcies were saleable, anybody should have his for fifty pounds"[96]: This is cash-for-a-title in a different key. Now that his wife has left him a wealthy widower, Mr. Elliot discovers that he values that title after all, and he schemes to secure it by marrying Anne.

Who deserves to live in the great house? Kellynch is rented to Admiral Croft, a hale man who made his fortune in the navy. It is notable that Austen's best gentry heroes, Knightley and Darcy, though not professionals, are still men of business. In the management of their estates they exhibit duty, discipline, and decisiveness, virtues that will be celebrated in and by the bourgeoisie and are embodied in *Persuasion* by naval officers. The latter are distinguished, however, for the degree of adventure and precarity encompassed by their profession. The financial proposition is not

96. Austen, *Persuasion*, 218.

merely uncertain; it entails mortal risk. In Austen's day, naval officers made their fortunes by scoring prize money. After the capture of an enemy vessel, every man aboard the victorious ship received a portion of the spoils, according to his rank. In its chanciness and brutality, the navy presented an extreme version of the society-wide shift away from fixed inherited roles and toward the vicissitudes of career as the life story of economic man. In this meritocracy, it was certainly not the rule that the meritorious went straight to the top; they could as easily go straight to the bottom (of the sea). To advance, a man needed not just skill and smarts but luck. And as in the tamer professions of church and law, connections were useful. In *Mansfield Park*, Henry Crawford, nephew of an admiral, secures a lieutenancy for William Price. Yet the navy men do not dream of being elevated (passive voice) in recognition of their merits. Wentworth's satisfaction is in having "earn[ed] every blessing that I enjoyed. I have valued myself on honourable toils and just rewards."[97] Success can fleet, as life fleets. The move from land to sea, from country house to warship, is a move from inheritance to entrepreneurship, from stability to volatility.

Except that landed fortune, too, is becoming chancy. There is no mortal risk in acceding to a hereditary estate, but it is possible to lose one, as by mismanagement compounded by social change. It is possible for the whole system to fleet, if the gentry and nobility are too obsessed with their own historicity to carry on their functions in

---

97. Austen, *Persuasion*, 269.

the present. *Persuasion* is relentlessly interested in the toll of time. Bath, the resort town to which Sir Walter repairs, "repress[es] the knowledge of growth and change, of decay and death."[98] Disconnected from nature, with only transients as occupants, it is a site of pleasure, consumer display, and eternal youth. Sir Walter, with his anti-aging measures, seeks to be frozen in time. But time passes and leaves its mark: in the crow's feet that emerge on Lady Russell's face, and in the eight years of romantic regret during which Anne has lost her bloom and Wentworth has made his fortune and—as it happens—marriage between a naval captain and a baronet's daughter has become acceptable to the landed and titled. Wentworth is "no longer nobody."[99]

Anne and Wentworth's marriage is very much of the moment, exemplifying and enabled by social change. It is not clear in *Persuasion*, as it is for instance in *Sense and Sensibility*, that the social order conspires against the meritorious individual and resists the formation of meritorious couples. That was perhaps the case when Wentworth initially won Anne's hand and Anne withdrew it because it was not the done thing. But eight years later, men of traditional rank are willing to be dazzled by men of naval rank. Society is becoming congenial to the capable man, in his professional and romantic aspirations. But there is no completed vindication. If the Wentworths' marriage is of the moment, their fortunes will partake of the good and

---

98. Wiltshire, *Austen and the Body*, 162.
99. Austen, *Persuasion*, 270.

bad of that moment. The meritorious couple must make its way in a world of opportunity and risk.

The ending of *Persuasion* stands out for its manner of withholding closure. It opens onto the present, which opens onto the future, which the author does not purport to foretell: "[T]he dread of a future war [was] all that could dim her sunshine. She gloried in being a sailor's wife, but she must pay the tax of quick alarm for belonging to that profession which is, if possible, more distinguished in its domestic virtues than in its national importance."[100] The present is the Napoleonic Wars, to resume just after the close of the novel's action in February 1815, with Napoleon's return from Elba. And the last war is never the last war.

Of course, not all of Austen's novels deliver satisfactory closure. Some arrange their marriages hastily and flippantly, or by resort to contrivance, with a metafictional self-awareness that presents happy endings as hollow forms and happy marriages as mirages. In *Northanger Abbey*, a viscount drops from the sky to marry Henry's sister, throwing the General into such "a fit of good humour" that he decides the humble Catherine might as well become a Tilney after all.[101] In *Sense and Sensibility*, the liberation of Edward requires a series of unlikely events, including Lucy's jumping ship and somehow getting hitched to Edward's younger brother, a development Elinor regards

---

100. Austen, *Persuasion*, 275.

101. Austen, *Northanger Abbey*, 260.

as "one of the most extraordinary and unaccountable circumstances she had ever heard. . . . [T]o her reason, her judgment, it was completely a puzzle."[102] No kidding. In *Mansfield Park*, Edmund relinquishes Mary for Fanny at an unspecified time, as suddenly and easily as one "learn[s] to prefer soft light eyes to sparkling dark ones."[103] Several novels leave bitter aftertastes. Elinor and Edward are still deprived of their portions, their oppressors remain on high, nor are the lovers "quite enough in love" to be reconciled to their straitened circumstances.[104] A paragraph in which Edward discourses "prettily" on his engagement ends in this way: "What he might say on the subject a twelvemonth after, must be referred to the imagination of husbands and wives."[105] Ouch! The ending of *Persuasion* presents a new problem: It does not end. The Wentworths' story continues as history continues, and in history all certainty and stability are contingent. The same psychological and social realism that persuades us of the Wentworths' happiness also imperils it.

Unresolved at the novel's end are all questions as to the meaning or tendency of the passing of time: whether social change is more for good or more for ill, whether there is anything to be regretted in the loss of those eight years, whether or in what sense, in Claudia Johnson's resonant formulation, "Providence has been equally served

102. Austen, *Sense and Sensibility*, 412.

103. Austen, *Mansfield Park*, 544.

104. Austen, *Sense and Sensibility*, 418.

105. Austen, *Sense and Sensibility*, 415.

by delay."[106] If *Persuasion* is distinguished by its conviction of the opacity of human affairs in both prospect and retrospect, it is equally distinguished by its several direct references to providence. Reflecting on her decision at nineteen to break her engagement to Wentworth, Anne regrets her capture by "that over-anxious caution which seems to insult exertion and distrust Providence."[107] Trusting to providence does not mean resting in the expectation of happy endings. We should have no particular confidence that Wentworth will rise to admiral as Anne cheerfully manages their prosperous household, to include five sons destined for brilliant careers and five daughters destined for brilliant marriages. Rather, it means resolution and resignation, without worry for the morrow. In *Persuasion*, providence displaces the happy ending as the narrative form of the good marriage. Marriage is presented as a departure, and the way ahead may be no easier than the way behind. Uniquely among Austenian couples, the Wentworths have no settled home at the end of their novel. They set out, like Adam and Eve east of Eden, into a world of uncertainty and violence, listening for the "quick alarm" of war. There is much to admire in their resilience, and much to anticipate by way of adventure. But they move through a fallen England. In *Persuasion* as in no other Austen novel, it is suggested that the only guarantee, in earthly terms, is the one acknowledged in their marriage vows: that death will part them.

---

106. Johnson, *Austen*, 166.

107. Austen, *Persuasion*, 32.

VII

Pride and Prejudice is everybody's first and favorite Austen novel, so it's not surprising that everybody reads the other novels through it. If Elizabeth Bennet marries brilliantly, so must Elinor Dashwood and Fanny Price and Jane Fairfax. If Pemberley exemplifies great-house Toryism, so must Mansfield, or it will be made to by the virtuous action of the heroine. Merit in portionless young ladies will be recognized. Nobody dies or is marked for death. All is light and bright and sparkling. But *Pride and Prejudice* is everybody's favorite for a reason that makes it anomalous: Its leading couple triumphs over darkness. Their triumph is distinctly the privilege of an elite.

Austen's most scintillating heroine, the dictionary definition of the meritorious portionless girl, makes the most glittering marriage. Mr. Darcy is the only Austenian hero whose suit receives explicit benediction: "He deserves you," says Mr. Bennet to his favorite daughter, whom he could not relinquish "to anyone less worthy."[108] Mr. Bennet's authority to bless a marriage is real but paradoxical. He has long declined to act the part of husband and father. He lives in his library and more relishes than deplores the carryings-on of his idiotic wife and such of their daughters as he can call "silly and ignorant." His patter is disturbingly funny, especially in his double-act with Mrs. Bennet, whom he "take[s] delight in" baiting.[109] His

108. Austen, *Pride and Prejudice*, 418.

109. Austen, *Pride and Prejudice*, 5.

constant theme is that the world is full of fools. His philosophy is stoical or cynical: "For what do we live, but to make sport for our neighbours, and laugh at them in our turn?"[110] He has never attempted to increase his income, though it is meager for a family with five daughters; he has very little to settle on them for dowries, or in the event that some or all end up spinsters. When the crisis comes— young Lydia runs off with the rake Wickham, and not to a chapel—his elder daughters turn to their Uncle Gardiner, a man of business. Mr. Bennet's contribution is to envy his brother-in-law "the satisfaction" of paying "one of the most worthless young men in Great Britain" to marry Lydia.[111] He regrets his failure to provide, and to that extent concedes that he is a moral agent. Yet we can hear him also saying, *This is all stupid; marriage is for fools.* A clever man stuck in the most unequal marriage in Austen, tethered to "a woman whose weak understanding and illiberal mind had very early . . . put an end to all real affection," he is an exponent of Austenian hatred in its purest form.[112]

As a figure of authority, Mr. Bennet embodies the paradox of cynicism: He takes misanthropy so far that it disables him as a moral actor and to that extent discredits him, but no one knows better than he that the world is dark and full of fools. The price at which he has purchased this wisdom becomes clear during his sole assertion of moral

110. Austen, *Pride and Prejudice*, 403.

111. Austen, *Pride and Prejudice*, 340.

112. Austen, *Pride and Prejudice*, 262.

agency, as he warns Elizabeth of the evils of the unequal marriage: If she is "unable to respect [her] partner in life," she will become demoralized and cynical; she will cuckold her husband and ruin herself; she is courting "discredit and misery."[113] If Elizabeth Bennet should meet the fate of Maria Bertram—what an end for such a girl! Mr. Bennet is wrong about Darcy, whom he takes to be Mr. Rushworth with a mean streak, but he is right about everything else. He perfectly enunciates the stakes of the unequal marriage, the false happy ending: It is a destroyer of merit. In this paternal exertion, Mr. Bennet far outdoes Sir Thomas. He has greater insight into darkness, and greater insight into his daughter's character, on the strength of which he is soon persuaded by her better information. We are not told what Elizabeth says about Darcy to effect this revolution: "enumerating with energy all his good qualities" is rather vague.[114] But we may observe that Darcy, like Elizabeth, is a good hater—that he strives to keep his hatred, like his pride, "under good regulation."[115]

In the great felicity it awards to one couple, *Pride and Prejudice* clarifies who is tops in Austen's spiritual gentry. "I am happier even than Jane," writes the newly engaged Elizabeth; "she only smiles, I laugh."[116] Though the Bingleys are happy and deserve to be, they are too "complying,"

113. Austen, *Pride and Prejudice*, 418.

114. Austen, *Pride and Prejudice*, 418.

115. Austen, *Pride and Prejudice*, 63.

116. Austen, *Pride and Prejudice*, 424.

too "easy," too "generous"—Mr. Bennet's genial judgment.[117] Mr. Bennet thinks well of Jane and Bingley, but he and we regard them a little condescendingly because they are too "blind to the follies and nonsense of others," unwilling to perceive darkness and hate the hateful.[118] Bingley's great defect (considered by Jane a virtue) is his diffidence. Darcy's famous defect is his pride, which likewise comes to be seen by a Bennet sister as a virtue. "By you," he tells Elizabeth, "I was properly humbled." His proper humbling has entailed learning "how insufficient were all [his] pretensions to please a woman worthy of being pleased."[119] These women make up a small cohort, one imagines, probably smaller than that of "accomplished ladies," of whom he has encountered six.[120] By recognizing Elizabeth's worthiness to be pleased, he confirms his own. Elizabeth finally acquits him of "improper pride," not of pride altogether.[121] The meek shall not inherit this earth.

Charlotte Lucas, who is often right even when she sounds wrong, proposed early on that "so very fine a young man … has a *right* to be proud."[122] To understand the conditions of Elizabeth's happiness, it is useful to specify how prestigious Darcy is—easily the most "illustrious

117. Austen, *Pride and Prejudice*, 386.

118. Austen, *Pride and Prejudice*, 16.

119. Austen, *Pride and Prejudice*, 410.

120. Austen, *Pride and Prejudice*, 42.

121. Austen, *Pride and Prejudice*, 417.

122. Austen, *Pride and Prejudice*, 21.

personage" in Austen, and not only among the heroes.[123] We are constantly reminded that he is handsome and tall, with £10,000 per annum; rich women fall into his lap (or try to); well read and with "a strong understanding," he is daunting even to his friends, per Bingley's complaint; he is masculine in a reserved style, with none of Wickham's generic jauntiness. As we shall see, he is an exemplary member of the great gentry. He is often called an aristocrat, which is just what he is not, for titles in Austen mark "mere stateliness of money and rank," corresponding to no "extraordinary talents or miraculous virtue."[124] In her view of nobles as frivolous at best, Austen betrays a bit of gentry snobbery. She carefully makes Darcy "as good as a Lord," with his Norman surname, noble forename, and near relations in the peerage, while preserving him a "plain Mr."[125] His untitled cachet evokes a commensurability of station and merit, according to the gentry ideology emerging from the eighteenth century—a time when the "endless creations" of junk titles by Whig parliaments added a sense of social fraudulence to the traditional critique of the aristocracy as a cradle of vice.[126] The "plain" gentry were on this view both socially and morally superior to the titled. Embodying such advantages, Darcy does not need to "recommend himself to strangers"—surely

---

123. Austen, *Pride and Prejudice*, 402.

124. Austen, *Pride and Prejudice*, 182.

125. Austen, *Pride and Prejudice*, 420.

126. Austen, *Persuasion*, 3.

one reason for Elizabeth's vivid resentment of him.[127] She can laugh at him, but she cannot laugh him off. Her eventual elevation will be not just to material fortune but to a stratum of the social order in which merit is rewarded, or at any rate distinction is lived up to.

Nor is it the case that Darcy is rude to the lowly. At least, he is no less rude to the lofty—and Austen is far from polite to his victims, who are people she hates. With one exception ("She is tolerable"), for which he pays in blood, Darcy is rude only to fools.[128] They range in status from Sir William Lucas of Lucas Lodge, an "empty-headed" knight whose fawning question about St. James's provokes Darcy to hint at a contempt for courtiership, up to his own titled aunt, whom he alienates for her insolence to his bride.[129] (According to his housekeeper, he is gracious to servants.) His rudeness to Caroline Bingley—freely confessing his desire for one woman, to another who openly desires him—verges on cruelty. Elizabeth later commends his sentiments: "You were disgusted with the women who were always speaking, and looking, and thinking for *your* approbation alone. . . . [I]n your heart you thoroughly despised the persons who so assiduously courted you."[130] We laugh at Miss Bingley's injuries because she is a snob who seeks to appropriate Darcy's prestige. His hatred of her is

---

127. Austen, *Pride and Prejudice*, 196.

128. Austen, *Pride and Prejudice*, 12.

129. Austen, *Pride and Prejudice*, 172.

130. Austen, *Pride and Prejudice*, 421.

exquisitely regulated—he is almost pedantic in expounding for her his admiration of Elizabeth's eyes—and we share it.[131]

Darcy can afford to "disdain . . . the feelings of others," low and high; the dependent spinster could only dream of doing so.[132] Darcy's cousin, Colonel Fitzwilliam, observes that Darcy acts just as anyone would who had his means: speaks and does as he wishes, comes and goes as he pleases. "Fifty miles of good road" is for him "a very easy distance"—an opinion that exasperates Elizabeth, for she has just endured those fifty miles between Meryton and Hunsford, confined in a carriage with that same Sir William and his tales of St. James's, to which she listens "with about as much delight as [to] the rattle of the chaise," because she cannot otherwise afford to visit her friend Charlotte.[133] Darcy's mobility allows him to depart any society he finds "confined."[134] Reading Harding's "Regulated Hatred," we might ask how Austen would have behaved had she not needed to cultivate rich relatives in order to survive, had she not needed to get along with whatever society was around wherever the Austen ladies were being accommodated. She might have behaved much as Darcy does. After their engagement, it transpires that Darcy and Elizabeth are of one mind concerning which of

131. Austen, *Pride and Prejudice*, 57.

132. Austen, *Pride and Prejudice*, 215.

133. Austen, *Pride and Prejudice*, 201, 172.

134. Austen, *Pride and Prejudice*, 47.

her Meryton connections they can interact with "without mortification," and Elizabeth can hardly wait to escape these people and constitute a new "family party at Pemberley."[135] This is one factor in the swiftness and completeness of Darcy's redemption: His hauteur is everybody's social revenge fantasy.

Since Darcy was damned early on for being "above his company" in Meryton, we may be surprised to find the novel commending removal as the higher civility.[136] But even the ingenuous Bingleys find after a twelvemonth that they can't take Meryton anymore and flee to a county neighboring Derbyshire, to be near the "satirical" Darcys.[137] In his "propensity to hate every body" (smilingly denied), Darcy was ahead of the curve.[138] Hatred should be regulated but is very often called for. Pemberley emerges at last as a mechanism for regulating hatred by sifting and disciplining its owners' social circle.

Pemberley is the nearest approach in Austen to the country house of Edmund Burke's dreams. Charles and Caroline Bingley agree that Pemberley cannot be had, by purchase or imitation. It is august as rent-a-halls like Netherfield are not. Unlike Mansfield, it possesses aesthetic and historic distinction. Unlike Sotherton, it is being kept up tastefully. Unlike Kellynch, it has a competent proprietor.

135. Austen, *Pride and Prejudice*, 426.

136. Austen, *Pride and Prejudice*, 10.

137. Austen, *Pride and Prejudice*, 26.

138. Austen, *Pride and Prejudice*, 63.

Its portrait gallery allows Elizabeth to behold Darcy's countenance and weigh her feelings and opinions about him. It also positions him as the latest in a long line of proprietors of Pemberley, a role he acknowledged while parrying Caroline Bingley:

> "What a delightful library you have at Pemberley, Mr. Darcy!"
>
> "It ought to be good," he replied: "it has been the work of many generations."
>
> "And then you have added so much to it yourself—you are always buying books."
>
> "I cannot comprehend the neglect of a family library in such days as these."[139]

Darcy more bats down the topic than takes it up, but he provides a fine if incidental expression of great-house stewardship with a basis in family piety.

Architecturally, Pemberley House alludes to the Burkean ideal of domestic stricture as the condition of true liberty. As the narrator dwells on its many large windows from which beautiful prospects of the grounds may be seen, Pemberley appears very unlike the prison-house of Mansfield. The point here is not, as at Lady Catherine de Bourgh's Rosings, the costliness of the glazing, but rather the house's orientation to the outdoors, its charism of openness amidst enclosure, foretelling Elizabeth's incorporation there. The landscaping, in which

---

139. Austen, *Pride and Prejudice*, 41.

cultivation accommodates spontaneity, calls for Elizabeth even more clearly. Indeed, Pemberley appears to us more grounds than house. Mrs. Gardiner would not insist on visiting if it "were merely a fine house richly furnished . . . but the grounds are delightful."[140] Elizabeth and the Gardiners approach the house through these famous grounds, admiring as they go. Their surprise meeting with Darcy occurs outdoors, and he pivotally walks with them about the grounds, pointing out trout-streams and investigating curious water-plants. The mistress of Pemberley will not be confined.

If stone walls do not a prison make, there is also a refusal to wall the garden. Unlike Mansfield, and like Donwell Abbey, Pemberley has commerce with the world. But Darcy's world is wider. Knightley works hand-in-glove with his steward, William Larkins; he brews spruce-beer; he wears leather gaiters. We witness his discrete (often discreet) favors to Highbury's poor, who are his friends. By comparison, Darcy is involved with Pemberley and its dependents at a remove. He writes "letters of business" and travels ahead of his party due to "business with his [unnamed] steward."[141] He has a reputation in Lambton as "a liberal man"who does "much good among the poor" while being rarely seen.[142] Knightley is a parish magistrate, Darcy the type

---

140. Austen, *Pride and Prejudice,* 267.

141. Austen, *Pride and Prejudice,* 51, 283.

142. Austen, *Pride and Prejudice,* 292.

to become an MP in a few years. He has extensive patronage in the church. He is lofty rather than earthy, more great man than good neighbor, but unlike Sir Walter Elliot or Henry Crawford, he handles his business.

Pemberley is big business—a crucial revelation to Elizabeth. "As a brother, a landlord, a master, she considered how many people's happiness were in his guardianship! How much of pleasure or pain it was in his power to bestow!"[143] Quite a quote: pleasure, pain, power. Darcy's £10,000 per annum commits him to an enterprise that unites business and pleasure, indoors and outdoors, today and yesterday, local and national, and involves him in responsibilities to the neighboring poor, to a train of servants, to the village, to the church, to his living family, and to his ancestors. As Fiona Stafford notes, "the continuing stability of England seems more assured in the figure of Darcy" than in the militia regiments that ostensibly defend the realm but in fact unsettle the communities in which they are billeted.[144] Primogeniture, which looked so bad on Edward Ferrars, shows Darcy to advantage.

So it is more fitting than may at first appear, Elizabeth's wry confession that she began to love Darcy upon "seeing his beautiful grounds at Pemberley"—and that the latter half of the final chapter is taken up with establishing who

143. Austen, *Pride and Prejudice*, 277.

144. Fiona Stafford, "Introduction," *Pride and Prejudice*, ed. James Kinsley, 3rd ed. (New York: Oxford U.P., 2004), vii-xxxii, xiv.

has visiting privileges at Pemberley and who does not.[145] Mrs. Gardiner staked her claim even before the engagement—apologizing if congratulations were premature, but "please do not punish me so far, as to exclude me from P[emberley]."[146] Her joke presages the disciplinary function Pemberley will come to serve. Caroline Bingley, "very deeply mortified" but wishing to "retain the right of visiting at Pemberley," pays off "every arrear of civility" to the new Mrs. Darcy.[147] Lady Catherine, who estranged herself from her nephew by averring that Elizabeth and her connections did not belong at Pemberley ("Your alliance will be a disgrace; your name will never even be mentioned by any of us"), soon enough "wait[s] on them" at a Pemberley very differently constituted than she could wish.[148] Mr. Bennet visits, with or without an invitation; Mrs. Bennet never visits, presumably too much in awe of her son-in-law. Kitty Bennet is often at Pemberley, Lydia Wickham occasionally; George Wickham is banned. Georgiana Darcy, the proprietor's sweet and shy sister, makes Pemberley her home, and the Bingleys are under thirty miles away. As the Darcys select their circle, including and excluding, conducting diplomacy, setting boundaries and conditions, we see what they value: sense, civility, and their own union. The Gardiners are awarded the final paragraph of the

145. Austen, *Pride and Prejudice*, 414.

146 Austen, *Pride and Prejudice*, 360.

147. Austen, *Pride and Prejudice*, 430.

148. Austen, *Pride and Prejudice*, 394, 430.

novel, the most welcome guests of all, as "the persons who, by bringing her into Derbyshire," had precipitated this most equal marriage.[149]

Pretty paradisal, except that another preoccupation of this chapter is how unreformed the fools are. "I wish I could say," writes the narrator, that the marriages of Mrs. Bennet's elder daughters "produced so happy an effect as to make her a sensible, amiable, well-informed woman for the rest of her life"—but alas. "As for Wickham and Lydia, their characters suffered no revolution": They continue to pile up debt, and he continues to rely on Darcy to purchase commissions for him whenever he runs out of rope. Lady Catherine behaves herself, but there is no suggestion that she is reformed in her snobbery. Likewise Miss Bingley, who sustains her flirtation with Darcy despite the minor impediment of his marriage. It is true that Kitty, mixing in "society so superior to what she had generally known," becomes "less irritable, less ignorant, and less insipid," and that poor Georgiana gains a bit of backbone.[150] But the fools are not improvable.

Elizabeth had earlier thought of the example she and Darcy might set, to "teach the admiring multitude what connubial felicity really was"—a droll expression, though in the event they got the felicity.[151] They only fail to edify the multitude. Elizabeth's Pemberley effects no correction

149. Austen, *Pride and Prejudice*, 431.

150. Austen, *Pride and Prejudice*, 427-28.

151. Austen, *Pride and Prejudice*, 344.

of the social order, no general propagation of civility. It does not rectify or justify. It allows one couple to have commerce with the world on its own terms. Nor are its happy solutions imitable. The Darcys are married by "special licence," we may say, and we may further observe how massive are the resources needed to sustain the exception: an estate so great, it is played in films by Chatsworth House.[152] Elizabeth need not recant her verdict, rendered at a dark moment: "There are few people whom I really love, and still fewer of whom I think well."[153] But she can pronounce it in a happier mood.

VIII

The Darcys' unparalleled felicity—their openness to the world while maintaining a high degree of independence from fools—depends on the particular source and style of their wealth: its stability, abundance, and charisma, from which they derive the wherewithal to break convention without being punished, and to select and discipline their circle. The Knightleys are in a weaker position. They are denizens of Highbury for good and ill, and given social and economic trends it seems likely that their leadership of that village will be challenged ever more in time to come. As for the Wentworths, the nature of their wealth exempts them from the social vicissitudes of the gentry and precariat,

---

152. Austen, *Pride and Prejudice*, 420.

153. Austen, *Pride and Prejudice*, 153.

at the price of subjecting them to more fateful vagaries. Across these three equal marriages we observe a decoupling of money from land in the hero(in)es' fortunes, as once-upon-a-time gives way to modernity, the landed estate declines, and social and financial volatility rise. Austen's final project, *Sanditon*, begins with a present that is already suffused with the future, one characterized by liquidity.

Mr. Parker is building the future on sand. He inherited a little estate near the village of Sanditon, but he has set out to remake Sanditon as a spa town specializing in medicinal sea-bathing and other nostrums. From landed estate to real estate: Mr. Parker is a developer, a speculator, an advertising man, a startlingly modern type. Our heroine is Charlotte Heywood, a young lady from a modest gentry family who live "a very quiet, settled, careful course of life" on their well run farm.[154] She is brought to Sanditon on holiday by the Parkers in return for a favor done them by the Heywoods. With Charlotte, we look askance at Mr. Parker and his venture. The proto-bourgeois virtues that in *Persuasion* began to align personal merit with worldly fortune are emptied out in Mr. Parker, who is all activity and no profession, finding "vent for his superfluity" in his unproductive work, a business that is mere busy-ness.[155] Sanditon represents consumer society, an economy based

154. Jane Austen, *Sanditon*, in *Later Manuscripts*, eds. Janet Todd and Linda Bree (New York: Cambridge U.P., 2008), 137-209, 149.

155. Austen, *Sanditon*, 192.

on "the demand for everything."[156] The demand has not yet emerged, as Mr. Parker is still seeking occupants for most of Sanditon's houses, but he is heartened by signs that the local economy is shifting from rustic productivity to tourism. "Civilization, civilization indeed!" he cries.[157] "All fixed, fast-frozen relations, with their train of ancient and venerable prejudices and opinions, are swept away, all new-formed ones become antiquated before they can ossify."[158] All that is solid melts into sand.

Extending *Emma*'s insight that hypochondria is a response to modernity, *Sanditon* takes several angles on the psychology of invalidism. Mr. Parker's two sisters share his "superfluity of sensation," and they "dissipate [it] in the invention of odd complaints."[159] Their brother Arthur justifies his indolence and gluttony on the basis of a nervous disorder: "The more wine I drink (in moderation) the better I am."[160] No doubt. "Nervous disorders are the Diseases of the Wealthy, the Voluptuous and the Lazy," wrote the eighteenth-century physician George Cheyne.[161] He

156. Austen, *Sanditon*, 142.

157. Austen, *Sanditon*, 160.

158. Karl Marx and Friedrich Engels, "Manifesto of the Communist Party," in *The Marx-Engels Reader*, ed. Robert C. Tucker, 2nd ed. (New York: Norton, 1978), 469-500, 476.

159. Austen, *Sanditon*, 192.

160. Austen, *Sanditon*, 196.

161. George Cheyne, *The English Malady: Or, A Treatise of Nervous Diseases of All Kinds* (London: Strahan and Leake, 1733), 158.

seems to have anticipated Mr. Woodhouse—and Arthur Parker. Discussing the former, John Wiltshire observes an "association of the nervous temperament or constitution with affluence," an association that would continue to emerge throughout the nineteenth century as an artifact of bourgeois leisure, a byproduct of the industrial age.[162] In that democratic era, psychosomatic performance was to trickle down the social scale. It is already doing so in Highbury, where the fashion for nerves is taken up by the humble Harriet Smith.

The critique darkens in *Sanditon*, as Austen anticipates a powerful commercial interest in the association between social prestige and poor health. Potential lodgers are assessed for their rank, their propensity to spend money on leisure, and their propensity to spend money on medical treatments—three aspects of one desirable social type. Sanditon peddles both the ailment and its cure, generating a discourse of diagnosis and remedy that is, as Tony Tanner observes, "all too contagious."[163] Sea air and sea bathing are "anti-spasmodic, anti-pulmonary, anti-septic, anti-billious and anti-rheumatic."[164] Characters accordingly complain of spasmodic bile and rheumatism in addition to the canonical complaint, nerves. Asses' milk is prescribed for

162. Wiltshire, *Austen and the Body*, 117.

163. Tony Tanner, *Jane Austen* (Cambridge: Harvard U.P., 1986), 262.

164. Austen, *Sanditon*, 148.

tuberculosis, tooth extraction for a headache. The irrelevance of cure to complaint is always striking, sometimes farcical, occasionally horrible. Susan Parker, the headache victim, has "had three teeth drawn" on the advice of her sister Diana, "and is decidedly better, but her nerves are a good deal deranged. She can only speak in a whisper—and fainted away twice this morning."[165] Diana's tone of breathless satisfaction suggests the accelerationist logic of fads and vogues. All too contagious: In Mr. Parker's plan for Sanditon, trends in hypochondria are recruited to the industries of leisure and consumption. A resort for the fashionably ill, Sanditon creates its own market by propagating illness, as market society will create consumers by generating their sense of lack.

Sanditon is a pungent manuscript, busily and savagely satirical, uncannily perceptive about social and economic change, ruthless in documenting the social uses of weakness, with a dark view of modernity. Language degenerates, as medical jargon acquires a commercial purpose that foils its healing purpose, and the advertisement of remedies becomes inextricable from the advertisement of maladies. National history and symbols are monetized: Mr. Parker takes Charlotte past "Trafalgar House—which by the bye, I almost wish I had not named Trafalgar—for Waterloo is more the thing now."[166] The names of naval victories that not long ago secured the survival of England

---

165. Austen, *Sanditon*, 164.
166. Austen, *Sanditon*, 156.

are redeployed for real estate ventures and appraised for their commercial appeal. Sanditon is a town of vacancies, its windows adorned with signs "To Let." Its potential residents are anonymous, interchangeable: In an episode of clerical slapstick, "two large families" of potential lodgers turn out to be one and the same.[167] Modern leisure and mobility are anti-social and de-racinating. Nothing is not corrupted, not English, England, healing, or home. What chance for the meritorious portionless girl, who wishes (as perhaps Charlotte does, for in this forward-looking fragment she seems something of a throwback to Elizabeth Bennet) to assert her lively mind, her proper pride, over against a bunch of grasping nullities?

We cannot know what chance there is for a Charlotte, since the manuscript cuts off even before we have properly met the long-heralded Sidney Parker, whose dry comments on his siblings' neuroses are amply reported and speak him a promising young man. Austen was four months from her death when she laid aside the manuscript; she had earlier tried the waters at Cheltenham Spa, to no effect. Day after day, she was yielding the sofa to her hypochondriac mother and making do with three chairs and a pillow, which "never looked comfortable," a victim of the hypochondriacs and their monetizers.[168] The *Sanditon* manuscript is the laughter of a dying woman at those who play at being ill, who seek status or gratification in a mimicry of what is killing her. In one mode of humor, she played at playing ill

---

167. Austen, *Sanditon*, 164.

168. Caroline Austen, *My Aunt Jane Austen*, 13.

herself: "Sickness is a dangerous Indulgence at my time of Life," she wrote in a letter sixteen weeks before she died.[169]

But the joke is on the hypochondriacs, in three ways. Endeavoring to avoid physical sickness, they contract a spiritual sickness; they imagine that they can avoid death, which is the one thing that comes to all; and in death, they dread that which is not dreadful. In all this, they make an idol of mortality. Death is among the most traditional targets of comedy, in part because laughter is our only mortal resource against it, our only natural means of denying it the tribute—fear and awe—that it claims. Austen knew grief; she was hit hard by the death of her father. But she hated lugubriousness and sentimentality as modes of bereavement. From this hatred arose a few notorious prose passages. Austen's letters contain moments of brutal truthfulness concerning—shall we say—expiration. In a letter of 1811, she exclaims over news of a battle in the Peninsular War in which ten thousand had died: "How horrible to have so many people killed!—And what a blessing that one cares for none of them!"[170] Then there is Dick Musgrove of *Persuasion*, a naval casualty, the more lamented as the living forget how worthless he was in life. Mrs. Musgrove is "out of spirits" one day, dwelling on the loss of her son. But the "real circumstances" are

---

169. Jane Austen to Fanny Austen, March 23, 1817, in *Letters*, 314.

170. Jane Austen to Cassandra Austen, 31 May 1811, in *Jane Austen's Letters*, ed. Deirdre le Faye, 4th ed.(Oxford: Oxford U.P., 2010), 200.

that the Musgroves had had the ill fortune of a very troublesome, hopeless son; and the good fortune to lose him before he reached his twentieth year; that he had been sent to sea because he was stupid and unmanageable on shore; that he had been very little cared for at any time by his family, though quite as much as he deserved; seldom heard of, and scarcely at all regretted, when the intelligence of his death abroad had worked its way to Uppercross, two years before.

He had, in fact, . . . been nothing better than a thick-headed, unfeeling, unprofitable Dick Musgrove, who had never done anything to entitle himself to more than the abbreviation of his name, living or dead.[171]

In the evening, we are shown the "large bulky figure" of Mrs. Musgrove, shaken by "large fat sighings over the destiny of a son, whom alive nobody had cared for." As though anticipating later criticisms, Austen maintains that, "fair or not fair, there are unbecoming conjunctions, which reason will patronize in vain—which taste cannot tolerate—which ridicule will seize."[172]

Both incidents appall Austen's critics and set her defenders scrambling. *Persuasion*'s disparagement of "unfeeling, unprofitable Dick" and his "large bulky"

171. Austen, *Persuasion*, 54.
172. Austen, *Persuasion*, 73-74.

mother is arguably the most unregulated expression of hatred in all of her writing. In Mrs. Musgrove's "large fat sighings," wit turns to ridicule, as mortal flesh is contemned and bereavement seems mere foolishness. If some truth is enunciated here, it must be that many people die without having proved their worth or justified anyone's interest in them, even their mothers'—a truth that is not lamentable but "a blessing." Death does not transmute the worthless into the worthy; to imagine it does is to make an idol of the dead, and of death. Austen's refusal of tribute gives rise in this moment to an especially harsh wit—perhaps reveals harshness as the essence of her wit, as though the dispelling of fond illusion, the exposure of the foolish and snobbish and subpar, always alluded to the finality of death, to the pointlessness of trying to like or love those who don't deserve it. In the matter of Mrs. Musgrove's large fat sighings, it is not clear whether Austen's art fails or surpasses itself.

Mercifully, this is not her ordinary mode. After all, she was not armed only with wit. As her private papers establish, Austen drew on more-than-mortal resources against death, in her orthodox Anglican faith. In the light of faith, the final irony is that "Death, thou shalt die." If death is not the king but a clown, then wit need not be death-dealing. In its ordinary operations, Austen's satire is salubrious. Her laughter, writes Harding, is a "means for unobtrusive spiritual survival" amidst natural and social evils.[173] Austen's wit is "inspiriting, salutary, therapeu-

---

173. Harding, *Regulated Hatred*, 12.

tic," observes John Wiltshire.[174] Mr. Parker might add, "relaxing, fortifying, and bracing." For indeed it is everything seabathing should be. After reading an Austen novel, "nobody want[s] spirits; nobody want[s] strength."[175] Austen's prose is "anti-spasmodic, anti-pulmonary, anti-septic, anti-billious and anti-rheumatic," anti-inflammatory, antioxidant, antibiotic, and probiotic. And if you live to see these claims contradicted in your own person, never fear, for you are past mortal ills.

174. Wiltshire, *Austen and the Body*, 220.

175. Austen, *Sanditon*, 148.

ACKNOWLEDGMENTS

A shorter version of this essay appeared in the August 24, 2023 issue of *Compact*.

ABOUT THE AUTHOR

Julia Yost is senior editor of *First Things*. She holds an M.A. in English from Yale and an M.F.A. in fiction from Washington University in St. Louis. Her essays on literature and culture appear in *First Things*, *Compact*, and the *New York Times*. She lives in New York City with her husband and four sons.

WISEBLOOD ESSAYS IN CONTEMPORARY CULTURE

Wiseblood Essays in Contemporary Culture offer in-depth interpretations of literature and art at large from a distinctly Catholic vantage point, while also championing and criticizing notable Catholic contributions to culture.

SELECTED TITLES

The Catholic Writer Today
Dana Gioia

Christopher Beha: Novelist in a Postsecular World
Katy Carl

"Everything Came to Me at Once":
The Intellectual Vision of René Girard
Cynthia L. Haven

How to Think Like a Poet
Ryan Wilson

Duty, the Soul of Beauty:
Henry James on the Beautiful Life
R. R. Reno

The Tragedy of the Republic
Pierre Manent

Death Comes for the Cathedrals
Marcel Proust

Poetry and Mysticism
Raïssa Maritain

Christianity and Poetry
Dana Gioia